Musty-Crusty Animals

Crayfish

Lola M. Schaefer

Heinemann Library

Chicago, Illinois

Customer Service 888-454-2279
Visit our website at www.heinemannlibrary.com

Designed by Sue Emerson/Heinemann Library and Ginkgo Creative, Inc.
Printed and bound in the U.S.A. by Lake Book

06 05 04 03 02
10 9 8 7 6 5 4 3 2 1

Library of Congress Cataloging-in-Publication Data
Schaefer, Lola M., 1950-
    Crayfish / Lola Schaefer.
        p. cm. — (Musty-crusty animals)
Includes index.
Summary: A basic introduction to crayfish, focusing on their physical characteristics, habitat, diet, and activities.
    ISBN 1-58810-513-X (lib. bdg.)   ISBN 1-58810-722-1 (pbk. bdg.)
    1. Crayfish—Juvenile literature. [1. Crayfish.] I. Title.
    QL444.M33 S3515 2002
    595.3'84—dc21

                    2001003281

Acknowledgments
The author and publishers are grateful to the following for permission to reproduce copyright material:
Title page, pp. 5, 22 H. W. Robinson/Visuals Unlimited; pp. 4, 8, 16 E. R. Degginger/Color Pic, Inc.; pp. 6, 10, 14L Gary Meszaros/Bruce Coleman Inc.; p. 7 Gary R. Zahm/Bruce Coleman Inc.; p. 9 Phil Degginger/Bruce Coleman Inc.; p. 11 A. Blank/Bruce Coleman Inc.; p. 12 Mike Couffer/Bruce Coleman Inc.; p. 13 C. C. Lockwood/Bruce Coleman Inc.; p 14R Bill Beatty/Visuals Unlimited; p. 15 R. Brown/Animals Animals; pp. 17, 19 Dwight Kuhn; p. 18 Daniel W. Gotshall/Visuals Unlimited; p. 20 Philip Gould/Corbis; p. 21 D. Lyons/Bruce Coleman Inc.

Cover photograph courtesy of E. R. Degginger/Color Pic, Inc.

Every effort has been made to contact copyright holders of any material reproduced in this book. Any omissions will be rectified in subsequent printings if notice is given to the publisher.

Special thanks to our advisory panel for their help in the preparation of this book:

Eileen Day, Preschool Teacher
Chicago, IL

Paula Fischer, K–1 Teacher
Indianapolis, IN

Sandra Gilbert,
Library Media Specialist
Houston, TX

Angela Leeper,
Educational Consultant
North Carolina Department
of Public Instruction
Raleigh, NC

Pam McDonald, Reading Teacher
Winter Springs, FL

Melinda Murphy,
Library Media Specialist
Houston, TX

Helen Rosenberg, MLS
Chicago, IL

Anna Marie Varakin,
Reading Instructor
Western Maryland College

Special thanks to Dr. Randy Kochevar of the Monterey Bay Aquarium for his help in the preparation of this book.

Some words are shown in bold, **like this.**
You can find them in the picture glossary on page 23.

Contents

What Are Crayfish?

Crayfish are small animals without bones.

They are **invertebrates**.

claw

jointed leg

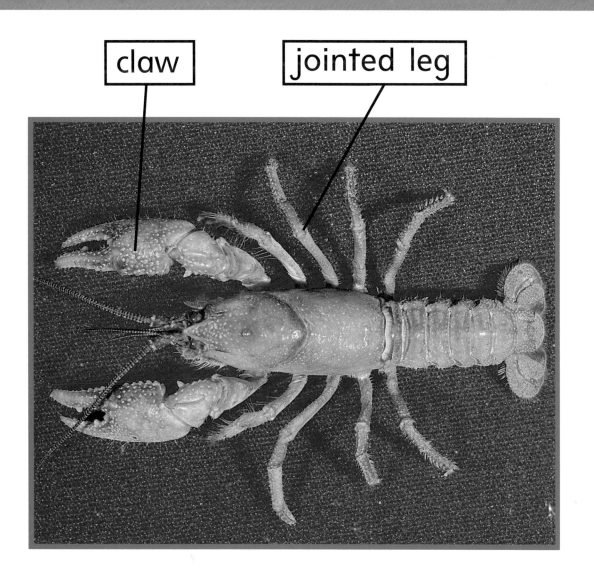

Crayfish have **jointed legs**.

The legs are for walking and holding food.

Where Do Crayfish Live?

Some crayfish live in rivers or streams.

Some live in lakes or ponds.

Some crayfish live on land.

They build mud homes in soft, wet dirt.

What Do Crayfish Look Like?

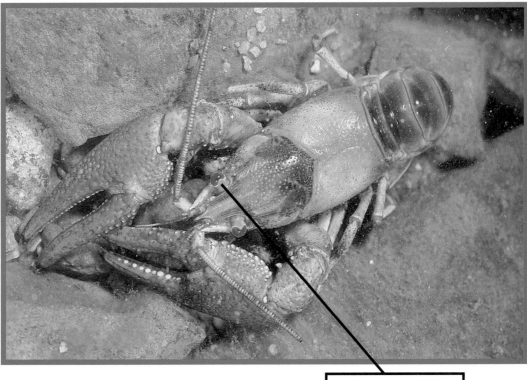

eyestalk

Crayfish look like large bugs.

They have two **eyestalks**.

antennae

Crayfish have **antennae** that feel, taste, and smell.

Crayfish can be brown, pink, white, or other colors.

Do Crayfish Really Have Shells?

People call the hard outsides of crayfish "shells."

But crayfish shells are really **exoskeletons.**

old shell

As crayfish grow, their shells get too small.

Crayfish leave their old shells and grow new ones.

What Do Crayfish Feel Like?

Crayfish feel crusty.

Their shells are bumpy and hard.

Their **claws** feel sharp.

How Big Are Crayfish?

Young crayfish are as big as thumbtacks.

Most crayfish could fit in your hand.

Some crayfish grow as long as cats.

How Do Crayfish Move?

Crayfish walk across land.

Their legs move forward, backward, or sideways.

Crayfish walk in lakes or rivers.

They walk along the sides or the bottom.

What Do Crayfish Eat?

Crayfish eat worms, fish, snails, and bugs.

They also eat water plants.

Crayfish eat dead plants and animals in the water.

Their **claws** hold, tear, and cut food.

Where Do New Crayfish Come From?

Crayfish lay small black eggs on their bodies.

They stay in the water with their eggs.

Little crayfish come out of the eggs.

They are called **instars**.

Quiz

What are these crayfish parts?

Can you find them in the book?

Look for the answers on page 24.

? ? ? ?

Picture Glossary

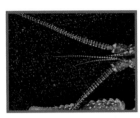
antennae
(an-TEN-ee)
page 9

instar
page 21

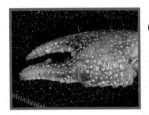
claw
pages 5,
    13, 19

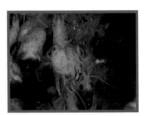
invertebrate
(in-VUR-tuh-brate)
page 4

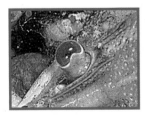
eyestalk
page 8

jointed legs
page 5

exoskeleton
(EX-oh-SKELL-uh-tuhn)
page 10

Note to Parents and Teachers

Reading for information is an important part of a child's literacy development. Learning begins with a question about something. Help children think of themselves as investigators and researchers by encouraging their questions about the world around them. Each chapter in this book begins with a question. Read the question together. Look at the pictures. Talk about what you think the answer might be. Then read the text to find out if your predictions were correct. Think of other questions you could ask about the topic, and discuss where you might find the answers. Assist children in using the picture glossary and the index to practice new vocabulary and research skills.

 CAUTION: Remind children that it is not a good idea to handle wild animals. Children should wash their hands with soap and water after they touch any animal.

Index

Answers to quiz on page 22

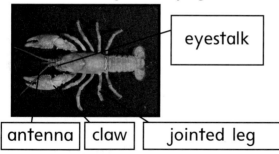

eyestalk

antenna   claw   jointed leg